My Faith, My Cancer, My God

How I Relied on God during My Darkest Moments

Betty Johnson

ISBN 978-1-63874-317-0 (paperback)
ISBN 978-1-68570-357-8 (digital)

Christian Faith Publishing, Inc.
832 Park Avenue
Meadville, PA 16335
www.christianfaithpublishing.com

Printed in the United States of America

To my Lord, my husband, my family, and the
wonderful doctors, nurses and health-care workers
who touch my life in such a special way

CONTENTS

Introduction

Thank you for purchasing my book. I wrote this book to give honor to God, for only He could have brought me through the most challenging experience of my life. There isn't anything special about me, and many of you may have gone through something similar or even worst. When I was growing up, I never heard the word *cancer*. It was described in so many other ways, but never cancer. The term was so closely related to death and hopelessness, no one ever called it what it was. Even now, the word *cancer* has a way of striking fear and dread in anyone's life.

And I was no different. I want to share my very personal story of my journey with cancer and of how God was with me and leading me all the way. I am sharing my journey with you to encourage, provide insight to anyone who may be going through something right now, or be witness to God's great love and mercy.

God is here for you.

CHAPTER 1

My Faith

Now faith is the substance of things hoped
for, the evidence of things not seen.
—Hebrews 11:1 KJV

Jesus is my hope, my truth, and my light. When I accepted
Jesus Christ as my Lord and Savior, I felt as though He
tapped me on the shoulder and told me now is the time to
make that public confession. I was twelve, maybe thirteen
years old at the time, and going to church was a requirement. I heard the Word at home and at church—that is, if I
wanted to go to heaven, I would need to repent and accept
Jesus Christ as my Lord and Savior. God is so good, and I
will tell you why. The first time I felt the prompting of the
Holy Spirit to join the church, I was scared. I didn't want to
walk down the aisle of my church alone, so during the call
to come forth, I just sat there, unable to move and fighting

the feeling that this was the time I should join the church. (In my church, an invitation was given every Sunday to the unsaved to give their lives to Christ and then make a public declaration by walking down the aisle of the church. Whenever someone gave their lives to Christ, there would be a lot of shouts and singing and rejoicing. The sinner saved by God's grace became the center of attention and would have to speak to the congregation about their salvation experience.) The following Sunday, once again, the pastor gave the invitation to come forth. I was prompted by the Holy Spirit to come forth. Only this time, God led someone else to join, and they went first. I said to myself, "Thank you, Jesus, I won't let you down." I walked down the aisle and proclaimed that I accept Jesus Christ as my Lord and Savior. God always makes a way for you and me.

"For God so Love the World that he gave his only begotten Son, that who so ever believeth in him should not parish but have everlasting life" (John 3:16 KJV). This is the Word.

The seeds of my faith were firmly planted by my aunt Amy. My aunt Amy could tell stories so vividly, I would feel as if I was there. My mother had eleven children, and she needed all the help she could get. So we would often visit and spend the night with my aunt Amy. She was a firm believer in God's Word. She didn't have any children at the time. Back then, there was only the radio, no TV, no cell phones, no phones. So telling stories at night became a favorite pastime. It is hard to believe in this high-tech world that such a time existed. We had very few material things, and yet the family values we were taught were priceless. As a child, my aunt Amy would make the Bible come alive for us, and she would often speak of Jesus's love and salvation. I can truly say she had a powerful impact on my life. Aunt Amy was one of the Mothers of the Church, very friendly, and she seemed to know everyone in the community. She had this crackly voice, soft-spoken, but she knew how to correct you when needed. A word from her regarding bad behavior would mean getting discipline from a mother. At church, if there was dinner being served, she made sure we would get a plate. Aunt Amy and her husband, Uncle Henry, loved children and played a big part in my life, as well as all my family. If she wasn't there, there was always my other uncles and aunts. Coming from a big family had benefits. Jesus was the center of our family.

Once I accepted Jesus Christ as my Lord and Savior, my faith became very personal to me. I could talk to Jesus anytime and anywhere. The Holy Spirit is dwelling in me. The Holy Spirit is likened to a river that runs deep in my soul and the essence of who I am. And like a river, it has ebbs and flows, but never runs dry.

I found that in my darkest hour, my faith in God, Jesus, and the Holy Spirit was what kept me going. Say amen if you know what I am talking about. I found that I could sit alone with the Lord and share my deepest fears, my hope, my needs. He knew them before I said anything. I could tell the Lord what I couldn't tell my husband, friends, or family. I wanted everyone to see that I am this fearless, faithful person, standing strong despite what I was going through. But God knew, and He kept my secret. I was being a fraud. He knew the real me, and he kept me strong.

I was trying to remember every Bible verse I have ever read, and I always went back to John 3:16 (KJV), "For God so Love the World, that he gave his only begotten son, that whosoever believeth in him should not perish, but have everlasting life." This verse was and is my foundation and defines the very person I am. For if I lived or died, God was with me.

I gained courage from thinking about the apostles of Jesus Christ. These men, being filled with the Holy Spirit, were able to carry on the work of Jesus Christ. Has Jesus changed? Has the Holy Spirit changed? Has God changed? No, God has not changed. He is the same God yesterday, today, and tomorrow. And that brought me comfort. I drew strength from the scriptures. When I read Genesis 1:1 (KJV), "In the beginning God created the heaven and the earth," I know that God has all the power, and His power has not diminished in any way. In fact, I am often reminded of Job. Job's faith was tested. Job had suffered much in that he lost all of his children, and then Job suffered an assault (illness) on his body. And at the heart of Job's suffering lingered the words "Why me?" I suggest to anyone who is going through something to read the Book of Job. I have learned to not ask myself "Why me?" but to ask "Why not me?" Job 38:1–18 answered the questions. I now know that God is sovereign and His will be done. The apostles of Jesus Christ were just simple men who learned to love the Lord with all their hearts; they learned from Jesus and remembered His words. They remembered John 14:16 (KJV), "I will pray the Father, and he shall give you another Comforter that He may abide with you forever."

Once I accepted Jesus Christ as my Lord and Savior, I was filled with the Holy Spirit, the same Holy Spirit that filled the apostles. Acts 1:5 (KJV) reads, "For John truly baptized with water, but ye shall be baptized by with Holy Ghost not many days hence." And Jesus did just what He said He would do. For in Acts 2:4 (KJV), it reads, "An they were all filled with the Holy Ghost, and began to speak with other tongues, as the Spirit gave them utterance." What God did for them, I believe he could do it for me. As I went through this journey, God manifested Himself to me in ways that I could never imagine. As my story unfolded, I could see God was way ahead of me, already making a way.

I grew up in humble beginnings (that's a nice way of saying my family was poor), but so were most of the families in my community. Our lives revolved around work, church, and family. I was taught the "Lord's Prayer" when I was child, and I said that prayer every night. It was a requirement. We always said our prayers before bedtime. I accepted the Lord Jesus Christ as my Savior when I was young. The only social gathering we were allowed to attend were functions involving the church, with the occasional school dance. As an adult, I wasn't always godly, but I never strayed far from the Lord. I married a man who loved the Lord, and we raised our children in the church. Let me make this very clear: we were not and are not perfect, but we serve a forgiving God.

> Forbearing one another, and forgiving one
> another, if any man have a quarrel against

any even as Christ forgave you, also, do
ye. (Colossians 3:13 KJV)

I am citing this Bible verse because it signifies what we should be to one another, and let me say this. One of the biggest hurdles in any relationship is forgiveness. Since I am normally an easygoing type of person, I found in my journey that forgiveness is something that I would have to deal with head on. And it is not always easy. I know in my head this is something I should do, but in my heart, I know I am not ready, and God would have to heal my heart. Sometimes the hurt just runs so deep, deep down in my soul, it takes time to process. It's not easy, I know, but it is necessary. I found that forgiveness was not about the other person; it was about me. I go down on my knees asking forgiveness from my Lord, so I know I have to forgive the ones who hurt me. My relationship with God became so much more than who I may think I am. If God says do it, I'm going to try my best to do it. I'm not saying it is going to be right away, but it's coming. God requires it. So I have determined no one can separate me from the love of God. Each of our relationships with God is unique.

As my story unfolds, I struggled with forgiveness toward my primary doctor and oftentimes became quite angry, and you will see why. Please read on.

I had to share how my faith played such an important role in my journey. God did it for me, and He can do it for you. Accept Jesus Christ as your Lord and Savior, and make John 3:16 your foundation, and grow from there, and be the very best you can be. God is waiting with open arms. Trust in the Lord to see you through whatever you may be going through. I cannot emphasize enough how a faith foundation can make a world of difference. That being said, let me share my journey with cancer with you. If you have not accepted Jesus Christ as your Lord and Savior, consider doing so right now. Will your problems suddenly disappear? Not likely, but what you now have is a God who will help you carry that burden. Jesus is the light that can shine through our dark days. Jesus said, "Come unto me, all ye that labor and are heavy laden, and I will give you rest. Take my yoke upon you, and learn of me; for I am meek and lowly of heart, and ye shall find rest unto your souls" (Matthew 11:28–29 KJV). What would be the takeaway for someone who does not know God. He will protect you forever.

CHAPTER 2

My Cancer

My journey with cancer actually started ten years earlier than my diagnosis. I had my scheduled colonoscopy when I turned fifty. I had the procedure, and the results were good—one poly that was benign. However, the recommendation was to return in three years. My primary doctor decided that since the poly was benign, I didn't need further testing for ten years. I had been with this doctor for over twenty years, and I trusted his judgment about our question. However, I started to have second thoughts about my doctor's judgment when I noticed other members of my family having colonoscopies every three to five years. Doubt started to creep into my mind. But I trusted my primary doctor and continued to see him. Hindsight is always twenty-twenty. I could tell you why I just didn't sit down with him and have a conversation. When I started to feel like something was wrong with me even though I felt fine, I knew I needed to make a change. I was going to make a change, but God was way ahead of me. Suddenly, my primary doctor decided he was going to retire and would end his practice at the end of the year. Thank you, Lord. I remember the name of a primary doctor who was actually considered quite good. This doctor seemed to go above and beyond what most doctors would do for their patients. I made an appointment right away. She was very thorough and reviewed my medical history, at least as much as what was available. I was fortunate in that all my doctors could share their patients' medical records (i.e., X-rays, test results, medical history and such). It was all in one place, so my new doctor would know what's going on with her patient. As my doctor reviewed my records, she stated I should have had a colonoscopy in 2009. It was now 2014. My heart skipped a beat, and fear came into my soul. She got me scheduled for a colonoscopy right away. Naturally, I took all this in with a smile on my face and left the office feeling dread.

Once home, I immediately began researching possibilities. I read everything I could regarding the colon and possible colon cancer. I would like to know what I would be facing. This was when that anger and unforgiveness seeped into my soul toward my prior doctor. I asked myself, *When did he become so arrogant in his thinking that he couldn't do what's right for me, his patient?*

Two weeks later, with my husband by my side, I went in for my colonoscopy procedure. I had been praying since I left my primary physician's office and knew from research that if a poly grew a certain way and it couldn't be removed during the procedure, a more invasive surgery would be required. I met with the gastroenterologist, the doctor who performed the colonoscopy procedure, for the results. I was speechless at first, and shaking inside, but I took the news well. I wouldn't let my emotions control me. On the outside, I took the news with grace and calmness. He had found nine polys. That's right, nine, and one had grown flat against my colon, so he couldn't remove it. I would need surgery, but he had placed a marker so that the surgeon would find it (X marked the spot). I didn't know they could do that. He would send the paperwork over and make the referral.

My husband was very reassuring as he tried to ease my fears. He had several surgeries, and this would be my first major surgery (other than the hysterectomy that I had a long time ago). I had been truly blessed with a measure of good health. He vowed to me that we were in this together and he would remain by my side. I smiled; I didn't want him to worry. We both knew I was in God's hands.

When I thought how this could have been avoided if not for the arrogance of my prior doctor, I became very angry. I considered myself an easy patient. I trusted my doctor to make the best decisions, and I made sure I always follow through on anything he recommended. He had not failed me before. But now this could be a life-or-death situation. I was not happy, but I could not dwell on my anger. I had work to do—pray and prepare for what was to come.

After meeting with my surgeon, who turned out to be a real dreamy, I felt so much better about my upcoming surgery. He was young, but not too young, muscular, and easy on the eye. He was thorough. He explained what the surgery would entail. I remembered how he explained that I could do anything except throw up. When I looked at him strangely, he explained that I could tear the stitches from the surgery, and he could not have that. I found out later how very serious he was about that after my surgery.

It was June of 2014; I went into surgery. My surgery was at the crack of dawn. I spent more time completing paperwork and making sure everyone would get paid by my health insurance than thinking about the actual surgery. But I was prayed up, and I wasn't afraid. God was with me. Once they finally got the IV in, it became a waiting game. My surgeon came in looking good, but professional. My husband made me laugh by commenting that he thought he could take him. I said, "Yeah right, it would be like Fred Stanford meets Rocky Balboa."

When they finally took me down to surgery, it amazed me that the room I was taken to looked like a broom closet, but it was there where I was given the medication that would put me out for the surgery. When I came to, it appeared that I was in a hall. They told me I would be in recovery for about an hour before being sent to a room. My husband and daughter were anxiously waiting for me when they moved me to a room. I was finally able to see my family, and I reassured my husband that I was doing fine, and at that moment, I was in very little pain. Once I got to my room, I was given a morphine drip. Once settled, I encouraged my family to go home since I wouldn't be doing much more than sleeping. The nurses and support staff worked twelve hours a day and were off every four days. So I wasn't sure if I would have the same nurse every day. And just like any other profession, some people did their jobs very well, and some did just enough to get by. I had a mixture of both. I found some people lingering and not doing everything they were supposed to do and waiting for the next person to pick up the slack. And that was the case after my surgery. I was covered in stuff and had lain in bed for more than twelve hours. I was ready for a bath and clean sheets. The first nursing assistant told me the next medical assistant would help me with getting a bath. However, I found that it was easier said than done. I was told they would bring everything and come back. Several hours later, I was still waiting. By the time I got everything I needed, I was in a snit. In my rush to get a bath, I got too excited and started to have dry heaves. This was reported to my surgeon. If I threw up, this could tear my stitches and he couldn't allow this, so I was placed on liquid diet. I felt like I was being punished just because I wanted a bath. And yes, I asked to speak to a supervisor, who did very little. My husband started to change the sheets when a very friendly nurse from a different floor stopped what she was doing to help change the sheets. God always places angels round you when you need them. She was my angel. I didn't get to eat solid food for three days. I cried when the nurse came in, and she called my doctor, who finally relented so I could eat. I discovered I was allergic to morphine, and I broke out in hives. I was placed on Benadryl. I couldn't sleep, but I got up and was walking. I did everything I needed to do because I was ready to go home. On my last night in the hospital, the new nurse told me I was prescribed medication to help me sleep. Are you kidding me? I could have been sleeping, and none of the other nurses bothered to get the medication. Shoot me now! Worst stay in the hospital ever. I survived because God brought me through this unpleasant ordeal. And I've come to realize that no matter how awful a situation I may be experiencing, someone else may be going through something far worst. God's word is food for my soul.

"Hear my voice, O God, in my prayer: preserve my life from fear of my enemy" (Psalm 64:1 KJV). The worst is over, or so I thought.

Once I got home, my husband had thought of everything, down to the little step stool placed by the bed to help me get in and out of the bed. We had at the time a very high mattress. He had cleaned, got the groceries. He tried to think of everything since I normally did the shopping, the cleaning, and the cooking. He was stepping into a new role, a caregiver. And he would find it a very challenging experience, not that I was difficult (I am sure he would disagree). It is just that being a caregiver, by its definition, is a difficult job. My hat off to all caregivers, for I believe you are blessed by God.

Two weeks later, I went back to see my surgeon. I felt good. He checked me up and was pleased with my healing. Then he dropped the bomb. The results of my pathology came back. I had forgotten all about that part of the surgery. I thought I was done. It was at this point he told me I had colon cancer, stage 3. It was possible that the cancer was in my lymph nodes, and I would be referred to an oncologist, the name of a cancer doctor. My mind was spinning. I walked out of his office, head up, smile on my face. My husband was in the car, waiting. Neither one of us expected bad news. After I got in the car, I just fell apart. He was confused and, while trying to comfort me, tried to understand what was happening. After a few minutes, I was able to tell him what the doctor said. He said we would get through this together. I dried my tears and put a smile on my face. I told him God will take care of me and take care of us. I had received many get-well cards from my church family, so I set them up on a small table as a reminder that God's people were praying for me. I knew God could do what the doctors couldn't do. But I recognized that God gave doctors and nurses and health-care workers the knowledge, wisdom, and skills to use them to help people. I often prayed for these special people even before I went to see them. It seemed that God was already ahead of me. Everyone thus far was very good at what they did. As I continued this journey, I would come to appreciate them even more because I had to go back to the hospital so I could get a port put into my chest to make it easier for me to get the chemo drugs, as everything would be administered by IV, as well as any blood taken to check how I would react to treatment. The only saving grace: it would only be a day surgery. Meanwhile, on the same day I went into the hospital for my procedure, my sister was also being admitted. She found out that she had breast cancer, and she would be having a procedure as well. We were being prepped on the same floor, in rooms next to each other. We consoled one another and made sure we were prayed up. The nurses kind of got a kick out of having two sisters on the floor at that same time, but we could keep each other company along with our husbands. See how good God is. We did well that day, although we would receive different kinds of treatments. I should also let you know our brother was diagnosed with prostate cancer as well. Our mother was in the early stages of memory loss, so she knew, but she couldn't stress for very long because she kept forgetting. I was relieved that she didn't have to carry that burden. God's word is always a comfort to me.

> God be merciful unto us and bless us; and cause his face to shine upon us. Selah. That thy way may be known upon earth, thy saving health among all nations. (Psalm 67:1–2 KJV)

My First Time Meeting My Oncologist

I tried to be prepared for everything, so I researched chemotherapy, medication, and side effects. But no one can ever be fully prepared. However, I wanted to be able to ask questions and have a clear understanding of what to expect. Like I said, God was already ahead of me. I was assigned a doctor I had never met, and I knew very little about him. So I was very surprised and pleased to meet someone who took his time and explained the process and even wrote down for me the type of medication I would receive. He spent at least an hour with my husband and me and showed us around the place. We were shown a large room with rows of recliners. I would be able to pick a chair that was vacant and make myself comfortable while getting the treatment. I felt everything would be okay.

During my first treatment, my vitals were taken, and then I was taken to the back. I found myself a recliner and settled in. I brought with me my Kindle, magazines, snacks, and water, although I found out that they provide water and snacks and such. They had these wonderful volunteers who would come around and make sure everyone was comfortable. If we needed a warm blanket, water, coffee, or snacks, they would bring it. This in itself freed the nurses up to take care of the patients. All the nurses were very friendly, and I had a very lovely nurse who hooked up my IV through the port that had been put in that main vein just above my heart so that I could get the medication. I was there for four hours. They would hang different bags of what had been prescribed for me; the first was something for nausea, and then the chemo drugs, etc. After I was done for the day, I was given a fanny pack of sorts filled with chemo drugs. I had to wear this for twenty-four hours and sleep with it. They provided a long tube so I could sleep. The next day, I would come back, and they would take it off until the following week. At the time, I thought I could handle this, but little did I know. By the time the second treatment came around, I was still feeling upbeat, but this treatment left me more fatigued than usual.

The Lord is my light and my salvation, whom shall, I fear? The Lord is the strength of my life of whom shall I be afraid? (Psalm 27:1 KJV)

By the third treatment, I could start seeing changes in my body. I had thrush in my mouth, which made eating difficult. My hands and face started to darken. To me, I had dead people's hands. My hair started to thin. It was already thin, and it got thinner. I wish it had fallen all out. But this was my cross to bear, and I wouldn't complain over my own vanity, and I knew there were others who were worse than I was.

After each treatment, I became weaker and weaker. My husband would often help me walk from one room to the next. After one particular treatment, I was able to go shopping with my husband and do different errands. It was a great day, but when we got home, I sat down and started crying. I was just thankful for such a good day. My husband became very concerned, and in the most caring and sincere voice, he asked me what was wrong. I can still hear that loving voice. So I pulled myself together and assured him I was fine. How blessed I am. I was seeing a side of my husband that was so loving. God had placed the perfect caregiver for me. Any serious illness can place a strain on a relationship. I have heard of husbands leaving their wives during difficult times of illness or vice versa. My husband and I had been married for forty years, so we had a strong foundation of love between us, and we have had our share of ups and downs, but we were always there for each other. Over the years, he has had several surgeries, and our roles were in reverse. Now he had to be the caregiver.

There were two times in particular when my husband came to my rescue. I had taken a shower and was going to the bedroom when I fell flat on the floor and could not get up. Too weak, I felt like I had fainted. He helped me up and got me to bed. We called the doctor, and he couldn't figure out what would have happened if I had been there alone. Thank you, Lord. The second time was even stranger. It was in the middle of the night. I just got up and went to the bathroom. I was trying to get back into bed, and somehow, I got tangled up in the covers and started to fall out of the bed. I just knew I was going to hit the floor. Suddenly, I felt myself being pulled up. At first, I thought God had reached down from heaven and was pulling me up and saving me from falling, but God used my husband instead. He pulled me up using the covers, so I didn't fall. I have to tell you we had one of those high beds with a big box spring and big mattress. It was pitch black in our bedroom, and I couldn't believe what had just happened. I asked my husband how he knew. He told me he watched me all the time. I didn't know if that was good or bad, but in this case, it was good. Enough about him. What a guy.

The thing about chemo is it kills good cells as well as bad cells. At some point, I had to start to get shots to help my body replace red blood cells every other week. I got very familiar with a PET scan, which would show if my cancer had spread. I would pray before, during, and after it was over. My PET scans were sometimes as long as my treatment. I was injected with dye and had to wait for at least an hour before the test could begin. Then I was placed in the scanner, which was very loud. No eating before the test, and I had to lay very still. I would pray and focus on the Lord.

I had healed from my surgery without any problems and with very little pain. So my focus was staying positive and fixing my eyes on the Lord as I would go in for treatments. It was such a blessing to share our cancer stories with each other. Each one of us has our own story to tell. Sometimes, I would share my story, and I would be looked at in amazement. At other times, I would look at them with amazement and know I serve a mighty God, although it was usually someone else who initiated the conversation. I was something of a loner. I would find my corner if it was possible and entertain myself. I would pack magazines, water, crackers, and my Kindle. Someone would offer me a blanket or snack, and I would be fine. Since I could recline, like many others, I would take a nap. However, when I was sitting next to someone in a sharing mood, we would share what our journey was thus far and praise God. At the Cancer Center, I met many cancer heroes, just ordinary people who got tagged by cancer. One special lady shared how she went through months of different treatments before they realized that she had stage 4 ovarian cancer. She was in Canada when a doctor from Africa took her by the hand and asked her if she would allow him to pray with her. I was shocked and blessed to hear that she found a praying doctor. And any complaints I had seemed very small. I believe that God places people in my life, although it may be brief, for a reason. I met another cancer hero, who was such a lively, friendly person, but she was having a hard time. She was diagnosed with breast cancer. She had surgery, and then she got an infection and had to stay in the hospital for another week. She also had a port put in for her chemo treatment, but nothing seemed to be working as it should. The nurses had trouble with her port. Her family would come in with her for support. We would chat away, and every now and then, her family member would chime in. At our next treatment, she was wearing a scarf. Her hair fell out after about two weeks of treatment, but she was trying to be upbeat about it. She told me she drove a city bus. She was so small; I couldn't imagine her driving a big city bus. I didn't see her anymore at the treatment center and often wondered what happened to her. Then about six months later, my husband and I was driving to the mall when alongside came a city bus. I happened to look up at the driver, and there was my friend, waving her hands and smiling down at me. I responded with a wave and excitement. I just knew it was her. There were other times when I was humbled by what others had gone through on their cancer journey. I had nothing to complain about.

I was a diabetic before the cancer. With the cancer and treatment, my blood sugar was off the charts. I started to get nerve damage in my feet and hands. My feet were the worst; it's like my feet had frozen, and then as they started to defrost, I would feel the numbness and tingling and sometimes burning. I was told this would go away once treatment stopped. It didn't. The treatments continued. I always tried to put my best face forward and smile when I didn't feel like smiling. I watched as certain patients and families handle this critical time in their lives. Sometimes a patient would have five or six family members come with them and stay with them for the entire treatment, which could be up to four hours. The most heartwarming ones were patients with their sons and their sons staying with them and keeping them company. Such devotion to their parent was a blessing.

Sometimes I would enjoy the solitude of the treatment. I could think and reflect without the world intruding on me, just me and the Lord, the good in a bad situation. Then as my treatment continued and the side effects of the chemo got me down, my anger would return, and I would think about my doctor, whose poor judgment put me here. Some of my fellow cancer patients who had heard my story suggested I get an attorney. I was thinking about it. This is where forgiveness must take place.

The Journey Continues

After about six months of aggressive chemo treatment, it was time for me to have a PET scan to determine if the cancer was gone. I took the test and followed up with my doctor for my results. I can say I was very anxious, and I prayed. I asked my family to pray. I asked my church members to pray. I had determined that I would fight this battle as long as God wanted me to. The doctor came in and asked me how I was doing but didn't delay with the results—I was cancer-free. Praise God from whom all blessings flow. I rejoiced. My family rejoiced, and my church family rejoiced. I would have to return every six weeks or so to get blood work and my port flushed. Thank you, Jesus!

I slowly regained my energy. My hair started to grow back, and my skin lightened. I started to feel good. I even started to exercise. I started doing a walking tape. With my Fitbit, I started to do ten thousand steps a day, two or three times a week, and I even started to lift weights. I was feeling good. After being confined to my house for so long, I was glad to be out the house. I was even planning our vacation. Then I started to feel a little chest pain, but I put it off because I didn't want to go to the ER. But after the third episode, I decided I would go get checked. So my husband took me to the ER; I got the works: blood work, CT scan. The doctor recommended I spend the night. Here I go again, feeling unhappy. My roommate snored and slept with her television turned on with the volume turned up. When she was awakened by the nurse, I had to ask her to turn the volume down. At least, she was very nice about it. The next day, I was given all sorts of tests: EKG, stress test, and MRI. A cardiologist came to see me to discuss the test results. Everything looked fine, and I would need to make a follow-up appointment. I was going to be released, and I could go home. Just minutes before I was to leave, the nurse came running into my room and told me the doctor who was to oversee my care while in the hospital needed to speak with me. He told me he saw a little something on my MRI. He was reviewing my scans and caught it. He suggested I see a pulmonary doctor right away, and they scheduled an appointment for one week later. I went to the pulmonary doctor, an older man, very nice, who explained what happened. He was going to get my records and then see at the next appointment what we needed to do. In the meantime, I contacted my oncologist and explained the situation to him. He scheduled me to have another PET scan. By now, it was time for me to see the pulmonary doctor.

The pulmonary doctor told me that he had reviewed all my scans, including the ones that had been taken about twenty years earlier. He explained in detail that what I had was possibly a scar tissue. I had previously been diagnosed with sarcoidosis, but it was in remission. He stated I should be okay. I was relieved. This doctor was retiring in July. I was blessed to have seen him. Before I go on, this is where I must say God was already in the plan and working ahead of me. It started with a dedicated doctor in the ER when he decided to take a second look at my scans. You will see why as I continue, but if you miss it, I will show you. This Psalm was food for my soul.

> The Lord is my Shepard, I shall not want.
>
> He maketh me to lie down in green pastures: He leadeth me beside the still waters.
>
> He restoreth my soul: He Leadeth me in the paths of righteousness for His name's sake.
>
> Yea, though I walk through the valley of the shadow of death, I will fear no evil: for thou art with me; thy rod and thy staff they comfort me.
>
> Thou preparest a table before me in the presence of mine enemies: Thou

anoints my head with oil; my cup runneth over.

Surely goodness and mercy shall follow me all the days of my life: and I will dwell in the house of the Lord forever. (Psalm 23 KJV)

My Visit with the Oncologist

I had passed the one-year mark since my cancer journey began. The oncologist told me my cancer had not only returned, it had spread to my pancreas, liver, and chest. I would need to start treatment again with an additional medication that get to the cells so small that they could not be seen. I knew the routine. Had it not been for the ER doctor taking that second look, which started a new chain of events, I might not be here. My blood work with my oncologist had been normal. After my visit to the ER, my doctor ordered a PET scan, which showed the cancer had returned and spread. God was already making a way. It was amazing to me how God worked things out.

I couldn't understand why God would allow me to get cancer again. (Keep reading.) I prayed He would deliver me once again. My deacon called me when I told him what happened. He stated that God healed me once, and He will do so again. I found comfort in those words. As my aggressive treatment began once again, I started to lose my hair, lose weight, and got darker and darker, weaker and weaker. For the first time in my life, I needed to get a blood transfusion. I still have the stuffed animal they were handing out to the patients that day. It's such a small thing, but I felt like the people cared. It made me smile. I had God on my side, and people were praying for me. There was no time for self-pity. I wouldn't allow it.

My husband and I planned our vacation and what we would do once I recover. I knew that as a caregiver, my illness was taking a toll on him, but he would never let me know. I kept all my regular doctor appointments. My primary care doctor stayed on top of my care and was kept informed of my progress. At one visit, she read to me the report she had received from my oncologist. Upon hearing my condition spoken allowed, I felt terrible. My cancer had metastasized to my pancreas, liver, and chest. It sounded terrible. I just never focused on the cancer, but rather I focused on getting well. She called me a rock star for the way I had handled everything. I didn't feel like a rock star, but I was trying to represent God, my faith, and my deliverance and always tried to smile when I could.

My second bout with cancer was a little longer. After my third or fourth PET scan, I was cancer-free, but I was on a one-year maintenance treatment of chemo, not as aggressive as my other chemo, but it would kill the smallest of cancer cells. However, it started to affect my kidneys. So after several more CT scans that came back clear, we decided to end that treatment, and I would return for regular blood checks.

I was left with some physical scars, as well as emotional scars, but I grew spiritually in wisdom and understanding and was filled with a great desire to tell my story and glorify God and help someone else go through their journey, whatever it may be. We are all going through some journey, and we must encourage each other. The physical scars were neuropathy in my feet and sometimes hands; hearing loss, more in my right ear than in my left. My hair thinned so much in some areas, it's almost bald. But I put cream on my feet and a wig on my head, and I praise God for delivering me from my cancer.

On the emotional side, there is always a fear that the cancer will return, but that fear is buried deep inside of me. It is human of me, but spiritually I know I am in God's hand, and He can deliver me or call me home. His will be done.

God told me why I got cancer again; it was for His glory. I am to be a witness to His power, love, and mercy. Praise God.

CHAPTER 3

My God

Testimony

I don't know why I got cancer and why God chose to heal me from my cancer. Some didn't survive, including someone I was close to, but I do know that God is sovereign. His will be done. I don't know all the answers, and I think that is by design. Eve made the mistake of disobeying God's Word by trying to know as much as He did. I believe God wants me to trust in Him in life and life eternal. And as I read God's Word, I take comfort from them. In Exodus 3:14, "God said to Moses, I am who I am. This is what you are to say to the Israelites. I am has sent me to you." There is no beginning and no end to God. God called this world into existence. And for anyone who are still filled with unbelief, just look around. Mankind still cannot explain all the mysteries of this world. Why would a sovereign God continue to love mankind with his loving care, grace, and mercy? As during the flood, His love for His creation allowed God to rid the world of evil mankind and start anew. He could have destroyed everyone. But He made a provision to save mankind forever by sending Jesus Christ to be our Savior and giving us eternal life for those who believe. Evil still exists, but someday it will not.

God is sovereign. God is the supreme authority over everything and everyone. Life from a human perspective can seem very unfair. But I accept that God is in control at all times. I may not understand the what, why, or when, but I have learned to trust God completely. He knew when I got cancer, he knew that he would save me, and save in such a miraculous way that I would be a living testimony. My life was and is in His hands.

When I was a child and even as an adult, I have always been afraid of dying. Having cancer, I was forced to look at death in the face. I came to understand what the apostle Paul wrote in Philippians 1:21 (KJV), "For me to Live is Christ, and to die is gain." I came to understand that when I die, my spirit will be separated from the body, and my spirit will go to dwell with Jesus in heaven. When Jesus returns, my physical body will be resurrected and joined with my spirit. I will have a resurrected body to live eternally with Jesus. I have work to do for the Lord.

As I write this, I was reminded of David in 1 Samuel 17:17–52, you know, the account of David and Goliath. David came on the scene of the Israelites trembling in fear of Goliath. He was a young boy, and his outrage that his kinsmen should be so intimidated was beyond anything he had ever seen. But his faith leaps out at me; his courage and his confidence that God could and would deliver him take my breath away, and I could do no less in battling my cancer.

At every turn, God had already made a way. I believe everyone—the doctors, nurses, administrators, financial aid, everyone God placed in my life—served a purpose. I was blessed, and I prayed blessing upon them.

And let me say this: cancer treatment is very expensive. When I was first diagnosed with cancer, I had private insurance with a $250 deductible, but each year thereafter, the deductible went up. By the time my treatment ended, I had a $2,000 deductible. The cost of the drugs was over $10,000 for each treatment, but praise be to God, I was able to get assistance. Health insurance for all people is so necessary. No one knows when they may be in need of medical services. Trust in God, and He will make away.

Conclusion

When I completed my treatment and was told I was cancer-free, I knew I had to share my story. My pastor told me I should give a testimony of my journey with cancer, my testimony of how God brought me through my journey. I eagerly did so. First, I wanted to publicly thank all my family and friends and church family for their prayers and consideration. I addressed my congregation, family, and friends and told my story. It was well-received. It was at that time I realized that my story is about salvation. So many people go through trials and tribulations without God or hope. My relationship with God was the foundation of my healing and likewise if I was called home. I knew that Jesus has already prepared a place for me in eternity. I also realized I should share with everyone. When I started my journey with cancer, I didn't know what to expect. I had to learn what to do and establish a routine. I tried to always smile in the midst of my journey. I smiled so much one day, one of the volunteers started to call me smiley. I didn't mind. I hope my smiles encouraged and put some people at ease. It was a difficult journey. But I found God always put the right people in my life just when I needed a little something.

I shared with one of my deaconess sisters that I was always cold, especially my hands. My hands were always cold. Some people didn't want to hold my hand or shake my hand. I wasn't offended. I knew my hands were cold. But this sister pulled me aside the following week and said, "I have something for you." She gave me this big bag, and I wondered what this could be. Inside was a small blanket or throw. It was soft and warm. I loved it. I use this blanket to this day. I sometimes carry it with me from room to room through my house. I put it on my bed, shoulders, feet. It is comforting. I realized that blanket is what God does for me. God covers me in His love, His warmth, His wisdom, and understanding. God hears and answers my prayers. Prayer is so powerful.

I forgave my doctor, whom I felt was responsible for me getting cancer. God requires that we forgive one another, just like He forgives us every day. God took care of me from the moment the doctor made a poor decision. I realized that we all make mistakes, and there was nothing malicious in his decision, just poor judgment. I guess I was just disappointed. This doctor had taken care me and my family for years, and he let me down. But God will never let me down. I may not understand what's going on, but I know I can always trust God.

I have lost some of loss of my hearing and my hair, and there's nerve damage in my feet. These are reminders of just how blessed I am and how God brought me. My cancer returned for the second time, and God delivered me to tell my story, and it is my prayer that my story helps someone else, and God will receive all the glory. At this time, I am cancer-free for more than two years; all the follow-up of my tests has come very good. But I am trusting that God will continue to take care of me in all things. God did it for me, and God can do it for you.

In 2020, six years after my journey with cancer began, God blessed me and my husband to take a trip to the Holy Land (Israel). We had been planning to take this trip for years, but there always seemed to be something on. So when the opportunity presented itself, we decided it was now or never. We started praying that God would bless us and cover us. We went with Chuck Swindoll, Insight for Living Church. And I prayed that we would be placed with a group of people whom we would come to know and make lasting friends. I cannot tell you what a wonderful group of people we were selected to join. We had a worship service every morning near the sites we would be visiting for the day. Our group will be forever known as Bus Six 2020. We walked, fellowshipped, and learned all along the way. We can now read the Bible with greater understanding and teach the Word of God with a renewed sense of purpose. God truly blessed me and my husband. Considering my health issues, it was indeed a miracle I was able to this. I am a living testimony to God's sovereignty and goodness, love, grace, and mercy. I could consider it to be a privilege to be able to share my story. I know you have one too.

I was reminded that God is too wise to make a mistake. My journey was to give God the glory, to share my story so that someone else may be encouraged, enlightened, and saved. While all our journeys may be different, God can and will take care of us. Matthew 5:15–16 (KLV): "Let your light shine before me, that they may see your good works, and glorify your Father which is in heaven."

acknowledgments

I would like to thank each and every person who had a role in my recovery—the doctors, nurses, health-care assistants, my husband, my family, and my church family.

about the author

Betty Johnson is a lowly servant of God. She was fifty-nine years old when she was diagnosed with cancer. She retired after thirty-five years on the job. She is married and has two adult children and a very big family.

She is from the rural area of Ocala, Florida, and currently lives in St. Petersburg, Florida.

CPSIA information can be obtained
at www.ICGtesting.com
Printed in the USA
LVHW041748100222
710655LV00002B/352